HARCOURT BRACE & COMPANY

Orlando Atlanta Austin Boston San Francisco Chicago Dallas New York
Toronto London

The gingerbread man hopped off the pan.

He called, "Run, run,
as fast as you can.
You can't catch me.
I'm the gingerbread man!"

The woman ran.
The man ran.

"Run, run, as fast as you can.
You can't catch me.
I'm the gingerbread man!"

The horse ran.
The cow ran.

"Run, run, as fast as you can.
You can't catch me.
I'm the gingerbread man!"

Oh, no! A fox!
And that was the end
of the gingerbread man.